Read for a Better World™

JOBS

A Look at THEN and NOW

PERCY LEED

GRL Consultant, Diane Craig, Certified Literacy Specialist

Lerner Publications ◆ Minneapolis

Educator Toolbox

Reading books is a great way for kids to express what they're interested in. Before reading this title, ask the reader these questions:

What do you think this book is about? Look at the cover for clues.

What do you already know about jobs in the past?

What do you want to learn about jobs in the past?

Let's Read Together

Encourage the reader to use the pictures to understand the text.

Point out when the reader successfully sounds out a word.

Praise the reader for recognizing sight words such as *to* and *the*.

TABLE OF CONTENTS

Jobs Then and Now

Jobs have changed over time.

THEN

People walked to work.

NOW

Some people drive to work. Other people ride to work.

What can people ride to work?

THEN

People found jobs in newspapers.

NOW

People find jobs on computers.

THEN

Workers used paper.

NOW

Workers use computers too.

THEN

Farmers used animals in the field.

NOW

Farmers use many big tools. A tractor is one of them.

What other tools do farmers have?

THEN

Most women worked at home.

NOW

Women work all over.

What would life be like if you had a job?

THEN

Many kids had jobs.

NOW

Kids go to school.

THEN

Many jobs were not very safe.

NOW

Jobs are safer.

New tools help workers today.

You Connect!

What are some jobs you know about?

How would work be different without computers?

How can you learn more about how people worked in the past?

Social and Emotional Snapshot

Student voice is crucial to building reader confidence. Ask the reader:

What is your favorite part of this book?

What is something you learned from this book?

Did this book remind you of any jobs you know about?

Opportunities for social and emotional learning are everywhere. How can you connect the topic of this book to the SEL competencies below?

Relationship Skills
Self-Awareness
Social Awareness

Photo Glossary

computer

field

newspaper

tractor

Learn More

Brett, Anna. *World's Coolest Jobs*. Oakland, CA: Lonely Planet Global, 2020.

Kalman, Bobbie. *Community Helpers*. New York: Smartbook Media, 2020.

Leed, Percy. *Technology: A Look at Then and Now*. Minneapolis: Lerner Publications, 2024.

Index

Photo Acknowledgments

The images in this book are used with permission of: © Prostock-Studio/iStockphoto, pp. 4–5; © Library of Congress, 6, 8, 12, 23 (field, newspaper); © bernardbodo/iStockphoto, p. 7; © VioletaStoimenova/iStockphoto, p. 9; © Everett Collection/Shutterstock Images, pp. 10, 14, 16–17, 18; © monkeybusinessimages/iStockphoto, pp. 11, 23 (computer); © oticki/iStockphoto, pp. 13, 23 (tractor); © Stígur Már Karlsson/Heimsmyndir/iStockphoto, p. 15; © Wavebreakmedia/iStockphoto, p. 17; © dear2627/iStockphoto, p. 19; © SolStock/iStockphoto, p. 20.

Cover Photographs: © Library of Congress (inset); © PeopleImages/iStockphoto (meeting)

Design Elements: Mighty Media, Inc.

Lerner Publications Company
An imprint of Lerner Publishing Group, Inc.
241 First Avenue North
Minneapolis, MN 55401 USA

For reading levels and more information, look up this title at www.lernerbooks.com.

Main body text set in Mikado a Medium.
Typeface provided by Hannes von Doehren.

Library of Congress Cataloging-in-Publication Data

Names: Leed, Percy, 1968–author.
Title: Jobs : a look at then and now / Percy Leed.
Description: Minneapolis : Lerner Publications, [2024] | Series: Read about the past (Read for a better world) | Includes bibliographical references and index. | Audience: Ages 5–8 | Audience: Grades K–1 | Summary: "How we get to work, how we find work, and how we do our work has changed a lot. With engaging photographs and text, readers will learn about how different jobs used to be"—Provided by publisher.
Identifiers: LCCN 2022037109 (print) | LCCN 2022037110 (ebook) | ISBN 9781728491516 (library binding) | ISBN 9798765603529 (paperback) | ISBN 9781728499420 (ebook)
Subjects: LCSH: Occupations—Juvenile literature. | Vocational guidance—Juvenile literature.
Classification: LCC HF5381.2 .L443 2023 (print) | LCC HF5381.2 (ebook) | DDC 650.14–dc23/eng/20220926

LC record available at https://lccn.loc.gov/2022037109
LC ebook record available at https://lccn.loc.gov/2022037110

Manufactured in the United States of America
1 - CG - 7/15/23